PLAY DRUMS NOW
THE ULTIMATE DRUMSET TRAINING PROGRAM

"PLAY DRUMS NOW 1.0: DRUMSET SKILL BASICS"

- **Skill Level:** LEVEL 1
  (No experience needed)

- **Estimated Time To Master This Book:**
  1-2 months (with regular practice)

- **Goals / Expected Results:**
  Well-rounded knowledge and skill base to play a drumset and easily pursue further drumming skills.

- **Next Steps After Completing This Book:**
  Begin LEVEL 2 training, with these books:

"PLAY DRUMS NOW 2.1: Sport / Rudiments"

"PLAY DRUMS NOW 2.2: Rhythms + Timing"

"PLAY DRUMS NOW 2.3: Drumset Grooves"

"PLAY DRUMS NOW 2.4: Fills + Drum Loops"

"PLAY DRUMS NOW 2.5: Playing With Songs"

TABLE OF CONTENTS

PART I: KNOWLEDGE

- INTRO / THE PATH OF DRUMMING - p.4
- EQUIPMENT AND SETUP - p.6

PART II: TRAINING

- PRACTICING - p.18
- BASIC TECHNIQUE - p.20
- INTRO TO DRUM RUDIMENTS - p.26
- RHYTHMS AND READING - p.28
- GROOVE BASICS - p.34
- FILLS AND DRUM LOOPS - p.38
- OUTRO / NEXT STEPS - p.42

© 2021 by Adam Randall

All rights reserved. No part of this publication may be reproduced in any form without written permission of the publisher.

ISBN: 9780984436545

INSTRUCTIONS FOR THIS BOOK

1) **Do your best!** -- this training is an OPPORTUNITY to learn and build your skills for the sake of having more and more fun on a drumset!!

2) **Read and learn everything.** Nothing provided here is filler, it's all important.

3) **Read all the instructions carefully.** They are a little different for each type of exercise.

4) **Stay in control and avoid mistakes,** by playing slowly and repeating stuff many consecutive times. This is how patterns are programmed into your muscle memory quickly. (See 'Ideal Practice Method', page 18.)

5) **Prioritize sound quality.** Remember that your goal as a drummer is to enhance any music you play with.

6) **Practice the techniques and physical skills like you're training for a competitive sport.** Drumming isn't really competitive, except maybe with yourself, but strength and speed are still very important in this craft.

7) **Rehearse patterns like you're learning to speak a LANGUAGE** - continue speaking all of it that you know to keep it fresh, as you continue to learn more.

8) **Go generally in order from beginning to end in this training,** to make sure you are comfortable with all the main foundations of drumming. Then you can skip around and make additional passes through the material, to improve your skills and speed in various areas.

9) **USE www.PlayDrumsNow.com for more resources.** There are lots of free lessons available, as well as song playlists and tempo charts.

PART I: KNOWLEDGE

THE PATH OF DRUMMING

WHAT'S GREAT ABOUT PLAYING DRUMS: EVERYTHING

Drumming is an incredibly fun art form that tends to enrich the lives of both the artists and the audience. The training involved in drumming gives you unique mental and physical skills that apply to many areas of life. And with regular practice, it's relatively easy to make fast, noticeable progress as an improving drummer!

Over time, your improvements can even be a source of self esteem and confidence. Being a drummer can also bring you into contact with cool people (like other drummers) and cool communities (like drum shops, drumming events, etc).

So, there are plenty of motivating reasons to pursue this instrument!

You might acquire a drumset with the simple goal of having fun playing it.

But in order to do that, you have to learn HOW to actually play with this toy! You need to develop the ability to **physically play it**, and you also need to know **what to play on it.**

Drumming skill has three main components:

- a sport
- a language
- an art

The overall goal for the 'SPORT' side of drumming is to develop strong playing abilities, with enough control to produce high quality sounds.

THE SPORT ASPECT includes technique, ergonomics, speed and power development in your 'drumming muscles', coordination, agility, and precise timing/volume/aim.

The overall goal for the 'LANGUAGE' side of drumming is to have a large vocabulary of sounds and patterns that sound good on a drumset.

THE LANGUAGE ASPECT involves several categories of 'vocabulary' you want to develop: rhythms, grooves, fills, and songs.

The more variety of vocabulary you are familiar with and can execute easily, the more fluently you can 'play the language' of the drumset.

The overall goal for the 'ART' side of drumming is to use creativity to blend the skills from both the SPORT and the LANGUAGE of drumming, to play new and awesome things.

GAINING SKILLS + ACHIEVING GOALS

Just by reading this, you're already making progress toward your drumming goals, because you're gaining important concepts about how to navigate the territory of drumset training. Now all you need to do is keep going from here!

This book will give you a healthy dose of drumming skill, and by the end of it you will probably be able to sit at a drumset and sound more or less like a drummer.

The next two LEVELS of the 'Play Drums Now' training program have much more material and training - LEVEL 2 includes about five books and covers the main topics of drumming in much greater depth, including song training. LEVEL 3 is a vast realm of advanced training topics, and can last as long as you wish to train your skills.

INSTRUCTIONS ARE IMPORTANT

If you follow the instructions in this book carefully, you will be playing drums immediately and will possess the knowledge you need to go further. You will experience effective training that gives you a great foundation of skill and will make you hungry for more progress!!

The instructions are usually pretty specific and carefully worded, so please read them all when you're using any exercises in this book!

INEFFECTIVE PRACTICING causes many hopeful drummers to quit or stagnate forever. Basically, humans have similar tendencies / instincts overall, and in the case of drumming:
Efficient technique AND the proper practicing approach are counterintuitive for most people.

TECHNIQUE and PRACTICING are both crucial components of success, so it's good to learn these well. Without the right guidance, most drummers encounter a couple problems: (1) their practicing yields a lot of mistakes and a little progress, causing a dislike of practice that becomes a downward spiral toward never practicing. And/or (2) their instinctive technique causes them to have a hard time advancing their speed, coordination, finesse, or accuracy.

The observation of this dilemma has been one of my main takeaways from 18 years as a professional drum instructor, and was a central motivating factor in producing these materials.

You can trust that this training path will lead you in the right direction. It is the result of the quest to build a perfect drumming curriculum. It is designed to train drummers in a well-rounded way, with ALL the needed skills and knowledge, to keep you highly motivated, AND to help you avoid common pitfalls.

The program develops drumming skills in layers, starting with an inner ring of basics and completing larger rings of skill on each advancing round.

This way, all the different areas of skill can be developed in balance with each other, which is the secret to having really satisfying skills at every level.

EQUIPMENT AND SETUP

EQUIPMENT YOU NEED FOR YOUR PRACTICE AREA:

- **drumset** (acoustic or electric or hybrid)
- **sticks** (a couple pairs for drumset, maybe also some heavier ones for practice pad - multiple pairs are good)
- **practice pad** (10-12" diameter hard base with a rubber top layer is ideal)
- **drum key** (for tuning drums and adjusting certain hardware components)
- **rug or carpet** (to keep your drums from sliding on hard floors, like a 4'x6' or 5'x7' utility mat)
- **headphones** (rubber-tipped earbuds or studio ear-covering style are ideal, since they reduce the external sound of drums)
- **device to play music** (and ideally a playlist)
- **metronome** (either an app or physical device)

OPTIONAL BUT REALLY USEFUL:

- **table or shelf** (for various small items and tools)
- **notebook** to keep track of ideas, tempos, etc.
- **music stand** (or any furniture to hold papers and books to read while playing)
- **mirror** (for watching your technique on a practice pad - highly recommended)
- **cool lighting / art** (to make your practice area more inviting / comfortable)

CREATE YOUR INSTRUMENT

When your equipment sounds really good, it's easy to PLAY BETTER. Your overall sound heavily influences your creativity and your playing quality.

Dialing in the parts and positioning of your drumset can be an ongoing project.

Drummers have a unique situation with their instrument: it's actually dozens of smaller instruments collected together under the name 'drumset'.

This means as drummers, we have more options, more flexibility, and more *toys* available than other musicians! (And unfortunately more to carry to and from gigs...)

You can increase the size of your instrument anytime you want, or even set aside parts for later when you want to go small. Saxophones can't do this! You've clearly chosen the right instrument.

 vs.  ?

4-PIECE DRUMSET   4-MILLION-PIECE DRUMSET

HOW TO CHOOSE A GOOD DRUMSET?

The most popular configurations on the market are 4-piece and 5-piece drumsets, with varying sizes of drums. (The number of 'pieces' counted in a drumset is simply the total number of drums, usually a snare, a bass drum, and 2-3 toms.)

Honestly as long as you avoid the lowest quality equipment, <u>you can't go too wrong with choosing a drumset</u>.* There's no minimum or maximum number of toms, and sizes aren't too important; generally bigger drums are capable of lower pitches and vice-versa. Plus your skills can translate across most any drumset, so maybe consider the following factors in your choice.

*(At least avoid the 'child-size' drumsets. They are cheap toys at best, not good for learning on.)

Get good quality cymbals. You can't tune cymbals, so select them well (or replace them) right away. Cymbals are one of your main 'voices' on the drumset! Good cymbals are amazing, expressive, and can last forever, so they're worth the investment. **You need at least some hi-hats, a crash, and a ride** to begin with, and a second crash right away is a good idea too. Generally you want your crashes thin and your rides thick. Hi-hats can vary (I like fairly thin ones).

Get strong hardware and a good pedal. This is important to (eventually) have so it will stand up to the abuse of playing gigs, and allows for reliable adjustments and more stable-feeling drums at home too.

Make sure you have good drumheads that are in tune. It's a good idea to have a seasoned drummer or a local drum shop help you with this part. Any damaged or cheap heads (i.e. NOT made by Remo, Aquarian, Evans, or a similar brand) should be replaced. Bad heads can sound terrible and discourage your progress!

BEYOND THE BASICS

Here are a few ideas to keep in mind for add-ons to improve / expand your drumset:

CYMBALS
- crashes
- splashes
- chinas
- cup chimes
- trash / stack cymbals
- additional hi-hats
- additional rides

DRUMS
- timbales (think reggae, salsa music, etc.)
- another snare
- mini-timbales (or bongos with synthetic heads)
- roto-toms

PERCUSSION
- cowbells
- woodblocks or plastic blocks
- hi-hat jingles

HARDWARE
- double pedal
- clamps for mounting toms from cymbal stands, rather than the bass drum (allows better positioning of drumset overall)
- clamps with boom arm (for additional cymbals)
- additional cymbal stands

ACCESSORIES
- cymbal bag, drum cases
- music stand
- stick bag
- drum dots / moon gels
- cymbal sizzles

SETTING UP YOUR DRUMS
AND PRACTICE AREA

Once you have your drumset, you're going to want to spend some time getting it configured.

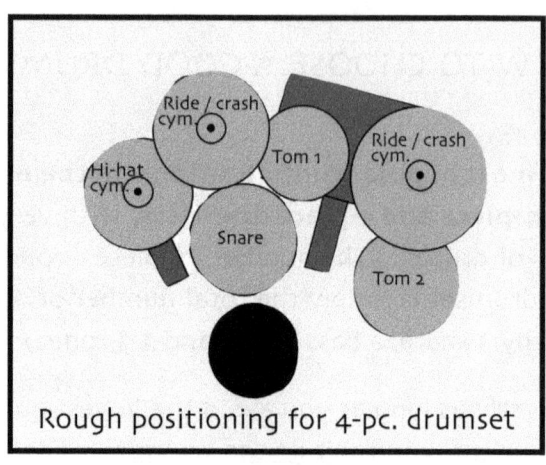
Rough positioning for 4-pc. drumset

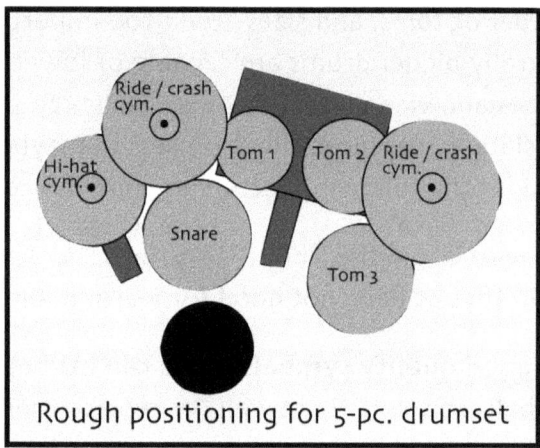
Rough positioning for 5-pc. drumset

DRUMSET SETUP ORDER:

1) **Start with the rug.**

2) **Adjust the seat height** so that when your feet are flat on the floor, your hips are <u>slightly higher</u> than your knees.

3) **Then add the snare** in front of the seat, and adjust its height so the top of the drum is <u>slightly above</u> the surface of your legs.

4) **Add your bass drum pedal and hi-hat stand**, and position them so when your feet are on the pedals, your feet are <u>slightly further away</u> than your knees.

5) **Attach your bass drum to the pedal** and add everything else, so it looks roughly like one of these diagrams (above).

6) **Adjust your drumset to be comfortable.** (see next section for info on making adjustments)

7) **Adjust your drumset to sound good** with tuning and muffling. (see next section for more info)

8) **Take it for a test spin!** Make more adjustments if needed.

9) **Add other furniture and lighting** (table or shelf, mirror, music stand, art on the walls)

8

EQUIPMENT ANATOMY / ADJUSTMENT

This section will serve as a complete guide for your knowledge, setup, and adjustment of drumset equipment.

5-PIECE DRUMSET

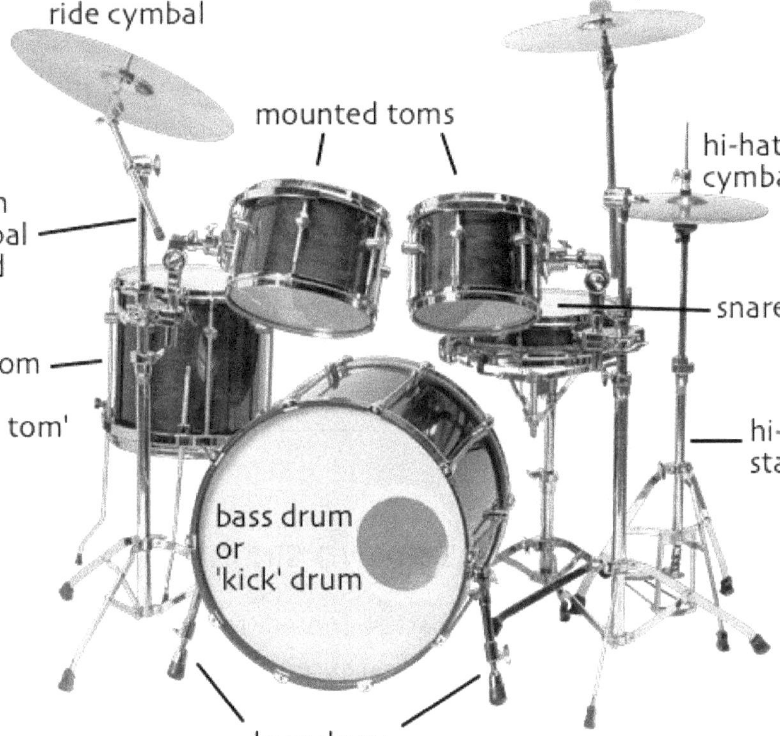

crash cymbal
ride cymbal
mounted toms
hi-hat cymbals
boom cymbal stand
snare drum
low tom or 'floor tom'
hi-hat stand
bass drum or 'kick' drum
bass drum spurs

ELECTRONIC DRUMSET

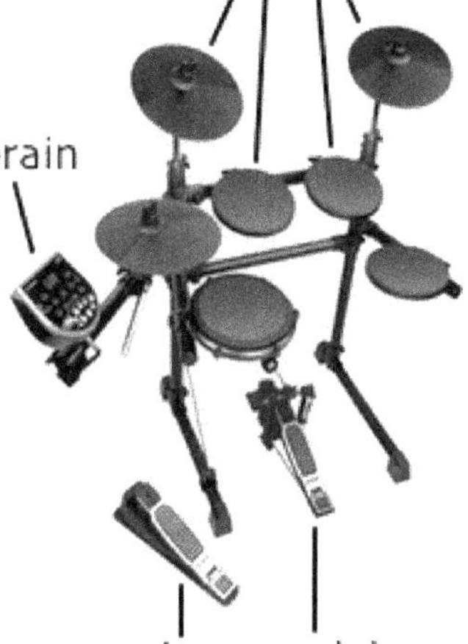

trigger pads
brain
trigger pedals

ANATOMY OF A DRUMSTICK

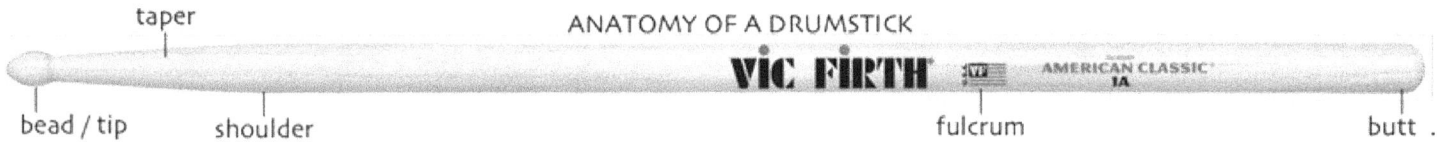

taper
VIC FIRTH
AMERICAN CLASSIC
1A
bead / tip
shoulder
fulcrum
butt

ANATOMY OF A DRUM

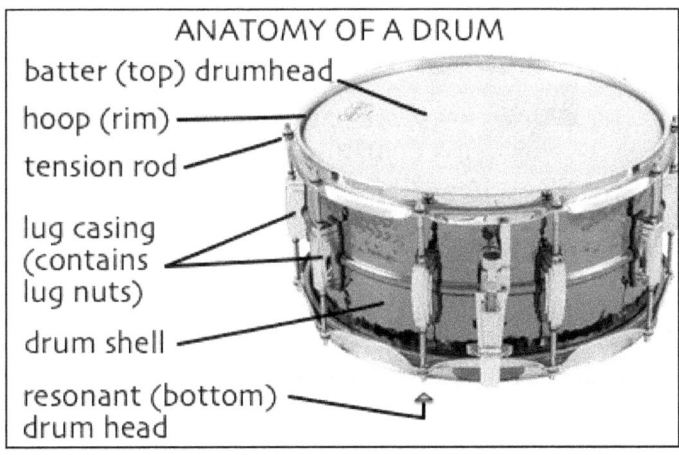

batter (top) drumhead
hoop (rim)
tension rod
lug casing (contains lug nuts)
drum shell
resonant (bottom) drum head

ANATOMY OF A CYMBAL

bell
bow
edge

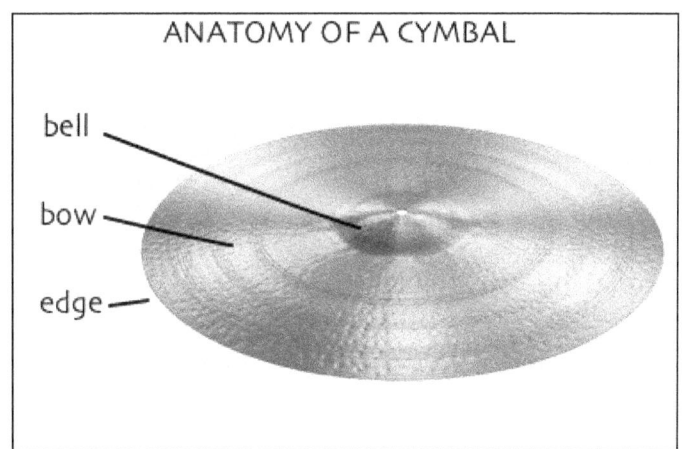

ADJUSTING HARDWARE

1. GENERAL STAND ADJUSTMENTS

Drum hardware adjustments are usually made by loosening a 'wing-knob' slightly to allow you to change the hardware's position, then tightening the knob again.

TIP: Make sure to support the weight of whatever is going to move with one hand while you loosen a knob with the other, so it doesn't suddenly fall or tip violently.

STEP 1: ADJUST THE TRIPOD BASE

Adjust the tripod so legs form a wide enough base to provide the stability you need.

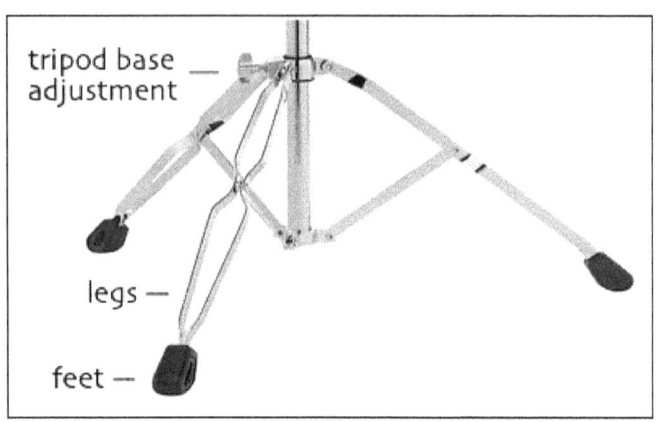

STEP 2: ADJUST THE STAND HEIGHT

If there is a memory lock, you may have to first move it before making an adjustment.

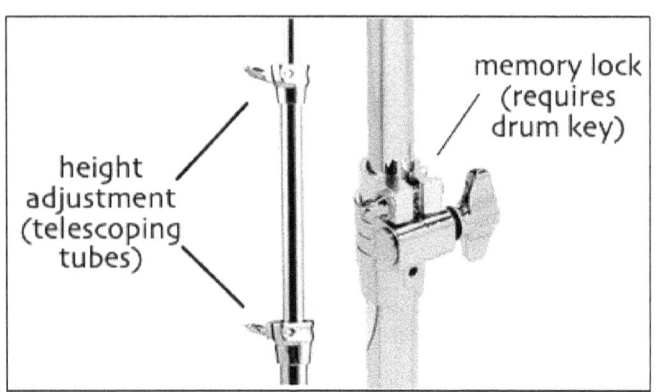

STEP 3: ADJUST THE ANGLES

Most stands have a similar angle-joint to control the tilt of your equipment.

TIP: When an angle joint has gears that fit together, wiggle the joint a little as you tighten the wing-bolt, so the teeth settle into place (otherwise, they sometimes end up resting tooth-to-tooth and slipping out of place later).

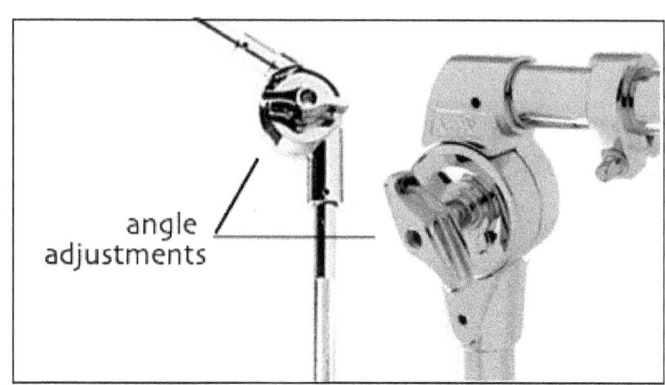

2. SNARE STAND SPECIFICS

Widen the basket enough to fit the snare. Add the snare, making sure the tips of the basket arms don't line up with the throw-off or butt plate of the snare wires. Tighten the basket so it grips the snare gently.

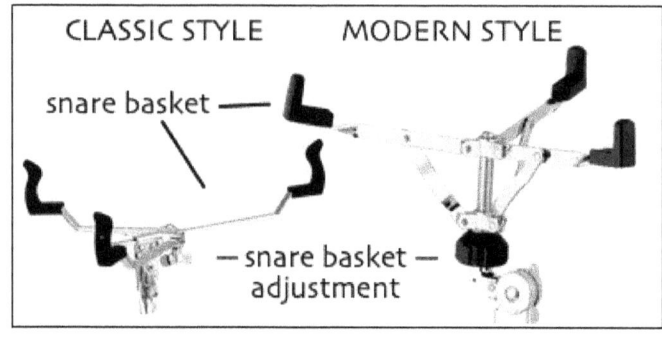

TIP: Adjust angle and height of snare to be comfortable (top of snare should be just above your legs when sitting on the drum throne).

3. HI-HAT STAND SPECIFICS

STEP 1: ADJUST THE STAND BASE

Make sure the pedal is connected to the stand base (if detachable). Adjust the tripod so that the feet AND the stand base make contact with the ground.

Also, make sure the pull rod is screwed in securely to the mechanism in the bottom half of the stand and moves with the pedal.

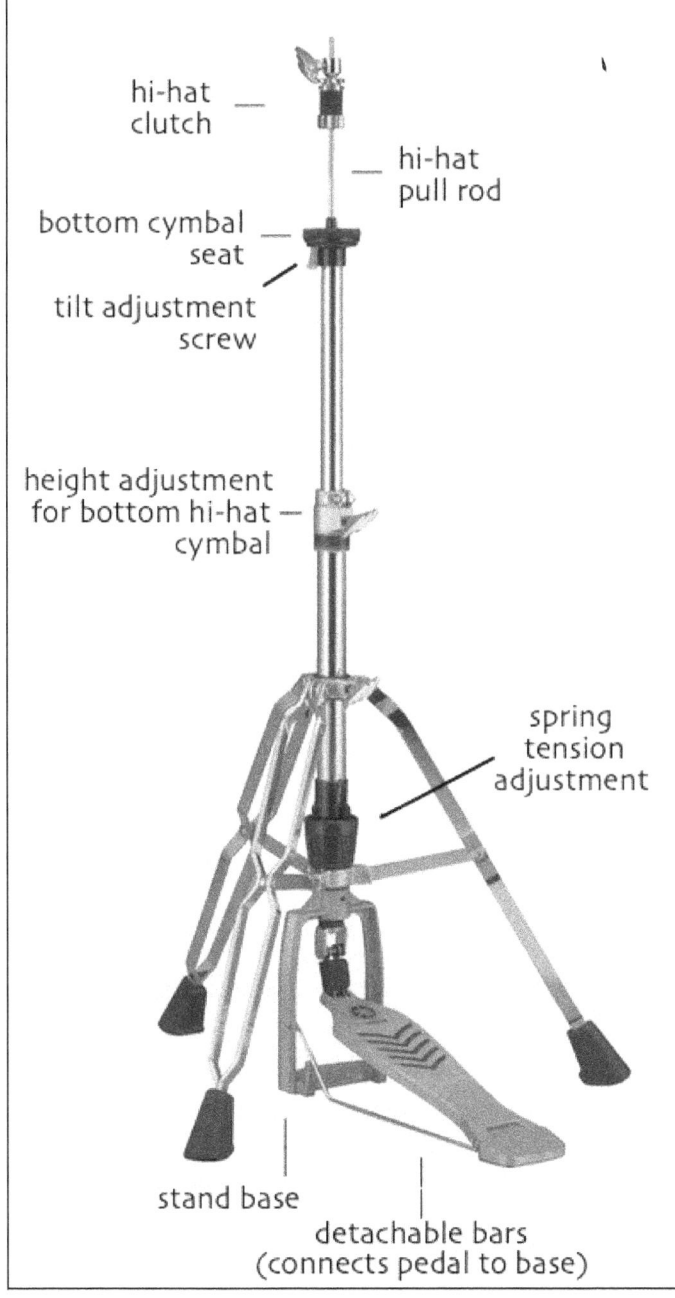

STEP 2: ADD THE CLUTCH

Attach the top cymbal to the clutch (between the felts) and tighten the 'lock nut' all the way until it stops, then adjust the 'compression nuts' (starting with the bottom one) to ensure that the cymbal is held tightly.

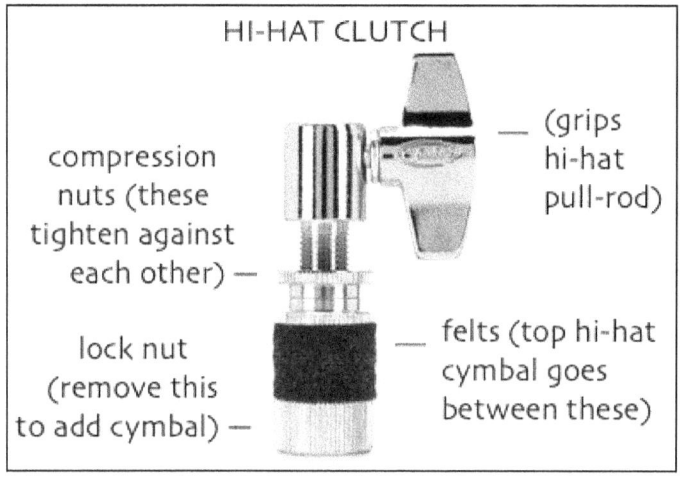

STEP 3: SEPARATE THE CYMBALS

Set the bottom cymbal height and add the bottom cymbal. Thread the clutch (with top hi-hat cymbal attached) onto the hi-hat pull rod and let the top cymbal rest on the bottom one.

Step down on the pedal about 1" and keep it there while you tighten the clutch's wing-bolt. The cymbals should separate completely when you let up on the pedal, but with only 1/2" to 1" distance between them. (You may have to adjust this a couple times, based on the spring strength of your hi-hat stand).

STEP 4: ADJUST THE TILT

Try closing the cymbals for the 'chick' sound, and if there is an air pocket being captured (the sound will be 'soft'), adjust the tilt of the bottom cymbal to create an angled contact between the cymbals.

4. CYMBAL STAND SPECIFICS

STEP 1: ADJUST THE TRIPOD BASE

Set the tripod so legs form a wide enough base to provide the stability you need.

STEP 2: ADD THE CYMBAL

Stack the cymbal between the felt pieces (make sure there is a sleeve on the cymbal post, or else cracks might start to form near the center hole), and tighten the wingnut just to the point where the cymbal has some room to breathe and move when struck.

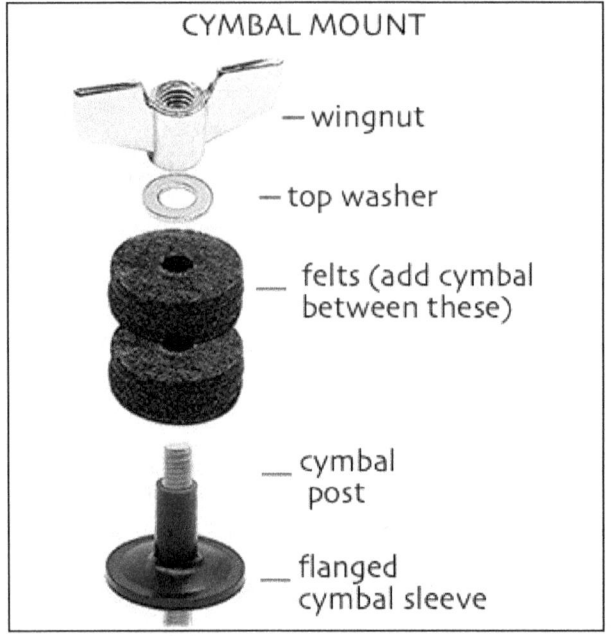

If you are using a boom stand: Adjust the boom arm to your desired length / angle, keeping the cymbal as close to the center of the stand as possible (first get the stand as close to your drumset as possible).

TIP: Make sure the boom arm is positioned over one of the legs of the stand for stability.

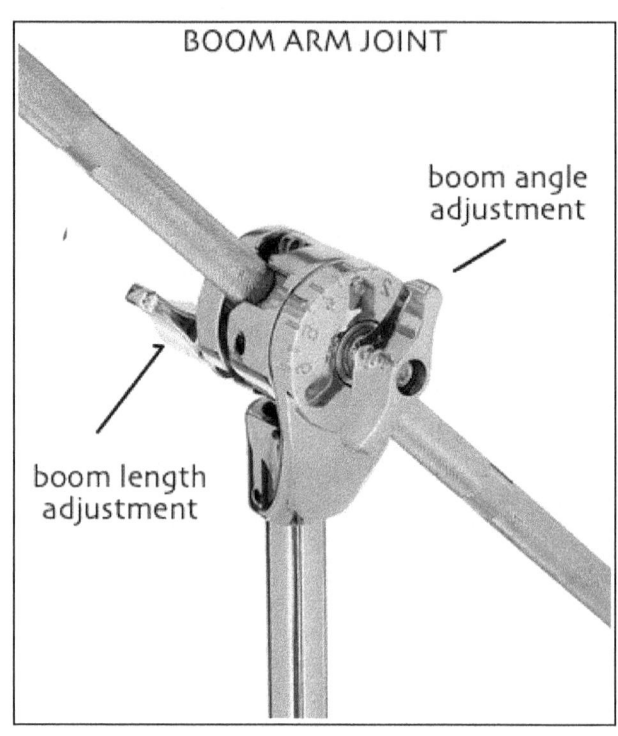

STEP 4: ADJUST THE TILT ANGLE

so the cymbal is easy to crash and/or ride on (see page 35).

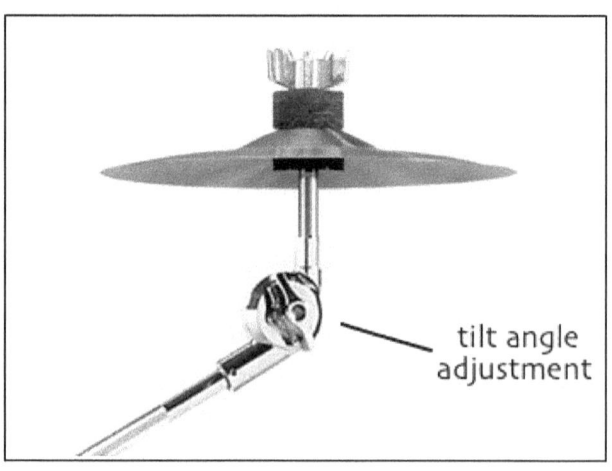

STEP 3: ADJUST THE STAND HEIGHT

Position the cymbal so it will have room to move without hitting your drums or other cymbals.

5. BASS DRUM / PEDAL SPECIFICS

STEP 1: ADJUST THE SPURS

Set the bass drum spurs to be equal length / angle, so the front end of the bass drum is off the ground about 1/2". For carpeted floors, adjust feet to expose spiked tips (if this is an option). DON'T use spikes on hard floors.

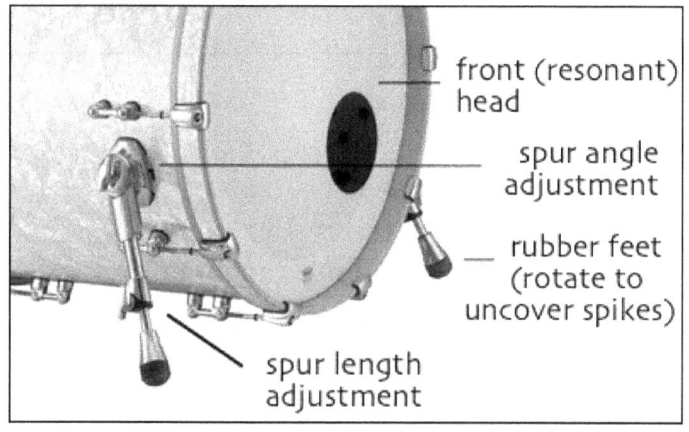

STEP 2: ATTACH THE PEDAL

Connect the pedal to the hoop on the batter side the drum, making sure it is centered and sits flat on the ground when connected securely.

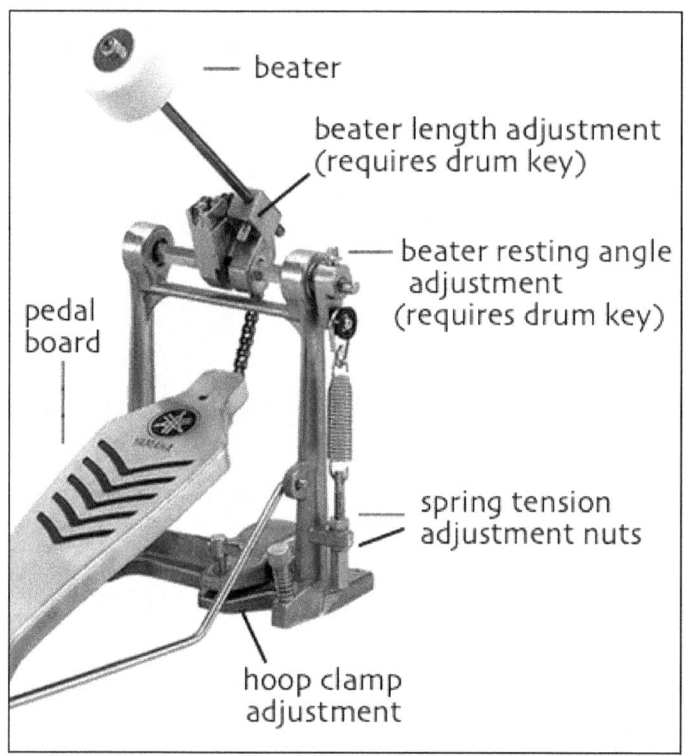

STEP 3: ADJUST BEATER

Check to make sure the beater impacts the bass drum head near the center, and adjust the beater length if needed.

Then, make sure the resting angle of the beater is comfortable (approximately 45° or so from bass drum head). Use a drum key to slightly looosen the bolt above the spring (see diagram), then move the beater forward or backward and tighten the bolt.

STEP 4: ADJUST SPRING TENSION

Adjust the spring tension to your liking - for reference, a 'medium tension' will cause the beater to swing back and forth about twice per second. Some drummers prefer more tension or less tension, so feel free to experiment.

To tighten the spring: Loosen the TOP nut first, and spin it upwards a short distance on the bolt. Now grasp the top nut and push the whole bolt downward as far as it will go into the metal tab, then tighten the BOTTOM nut to secure the bolt.

To loosen the spring: Loosen the BOTTOM nut first, and spin it downwards a short distance on the bolt (it helps to hold the top nut down against the metal tab while you do this). Now spin the TOP nut downward against the metal tab and tighten it to secure the bolt.

6. TOM MOUNTING SPECIFICS

STEP 1: ATTACH TOM ARMS

Insert tom arms (with joints set to about 90°) into bass drum (or into clamps on cymbal or tom stand).

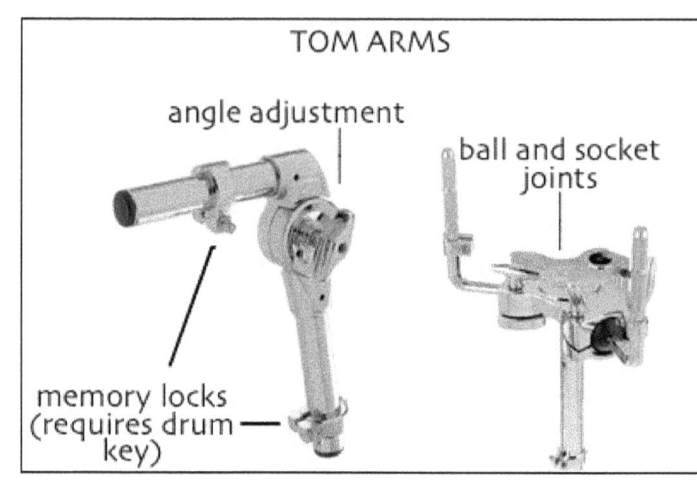

TOM ARMS
- angle adjustment
- ball and socket joints
- memory locks (requires drum key)

STEP 2: ADD TOMS AND ADJUST POSITION

Mount toms by attaching their mounting brackets to the tom arms, and tighten wing-knobs on the mounting brackets to secure toms in place.

Adjust angle and height of toms to your preference.

Make sure your toms are not too close to the top of your bass drum, or they will rattle and probably damage the exterior of your bass drum.

STEP 3: ADD FLOOR TOM(S)

With the floor tom upside down on the ground, insert the legs into the mounting brackets on the sides of the drum, with the angled parts of the legs facing away from the drum for stability. Tighten the wing-knobs to secure them in place.

Turn the drum over and place it where you prefer with your drumset, then make any final adjustments to the legs.

TOMS MOUNTED ON BASS DRUM

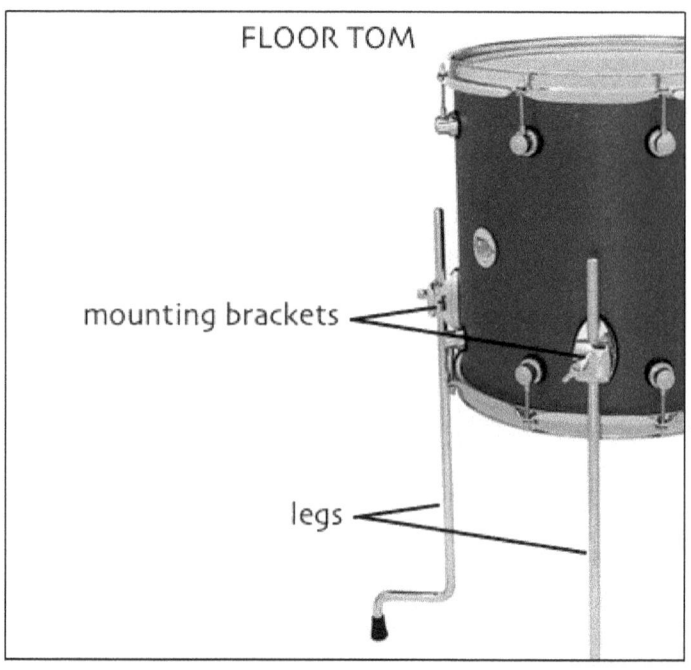

FLOOR TOM
- mounting brackets
- legs

7. SNARE WIRE SPECIFICS

STEP 1: ADJUST THE TENSION KNOB

Make sure the throw-off arm is turned on, and hit the snare's top (batter) head to check the sound.

If the wires sound too 'tight / choked', turn the snares off and loosen the 'snare tension knob', then turn them on and test again.

If the sound is too loose, turn the snare wires off and tighten the knob, then turn the wires back on and test.

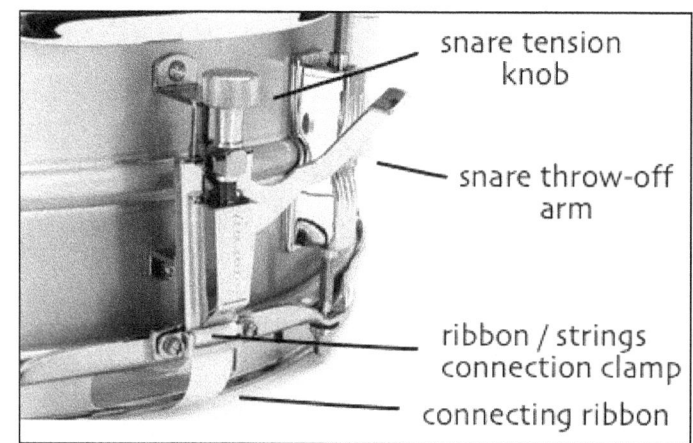

STEP 2: CHECK FOR ISSUES

Sometimes, the tension adjustment knob is screwed in all the way but the snares aren't tight enough to make a good sound. Or it's screwed out all the way, but the snares won't turn off.

Or maybe, the wires are off-center on the bottom head.

If any of these conditions is true of your snare, it's time to adjust the wires! Don't worry, it's easy.

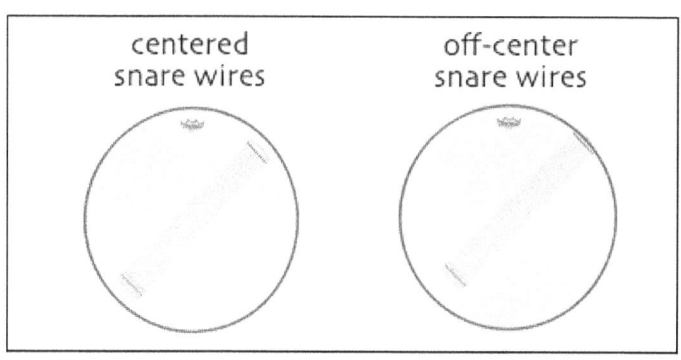

STEP 3: ADJUST THE SNARE WIRES

1) Turn off the snares (and make sure the snare tension knob is about halfway unscrewed), and flip the snare over.

2) Loosen the snare connection clamps at BOTH the butt plate AND the throw off, and center the snare wires on the head.

3) Take up any slack in the ribbon/strings and tighten the snare wire connection on the butt-plate side, then do the same on the throw-off side.

4) Adjust the snare tension knob (see STEP 1 at the top of this page).

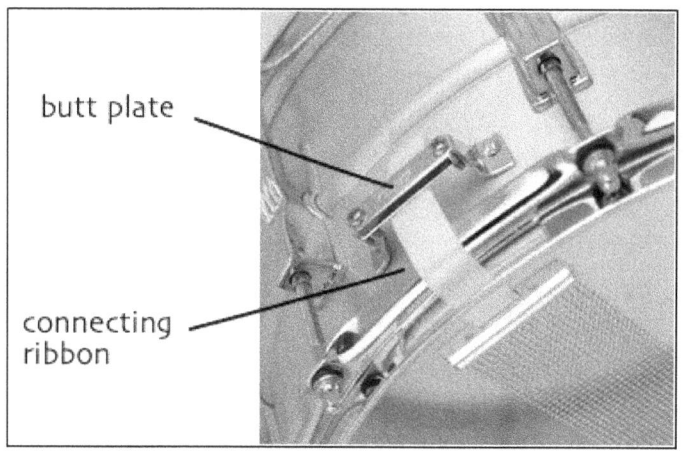

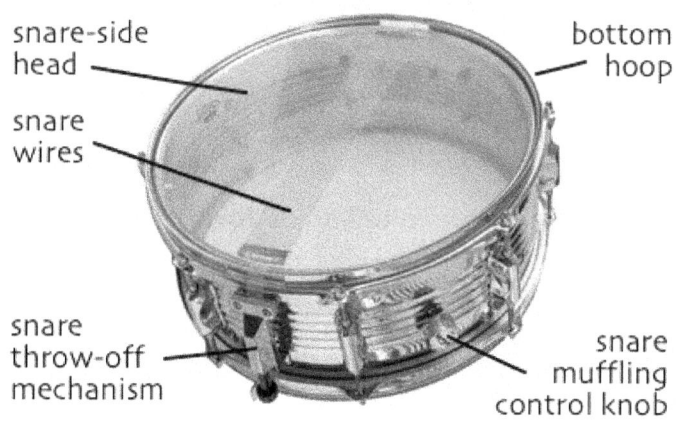

REPLACING AND TUNING DRUMHEADS

IDEALLY you'll want to have an expert do this if possible, but no problem if not. It's not hard to do a decent job of tuning drums on your own!

RULE #1 - Remove any drums from their mounts and place on a carpeted surface or towel before tuning.

This is done to mute the bottom head while you tune the top, so you can hear one head at a time.

RULE #2 - Tighten the heads roughly to a medium tightness, then tune by ear.

Basically, you want drumheads to easily move 1/2" - 1" or so when you push down on the middle. Try pushing on the head with your thumb near each tension rod, to feel for any major differences in tension. Fix those by loosening or tightening as needed, to bring the head 'roughly' into balance with itself.

Then, tap the head with a drumstick near each tension rod and LISTEN to the differences in sound. If you can detect a weak or lower-pitch area compared to the other areas, tune it up a little, until the head sounds more in tune with itself.

RULE #3 - Make small adjustments and balance them out before making more.

You might give a tension rod a quarter-turn or half-turn before adjusting the others, whether loosening or tightening.

RULE #4 - Keep all the tension balanced around the drumhead.

If you tighten a tension rod, then also tighten the one across the drumhead from it in the same 'pair'. Then tighten the other <u>pairs</u> of tension rods similarly. Here are the ideal patterns for tuning various drums (pairs are labeled A,B,C, etc.):

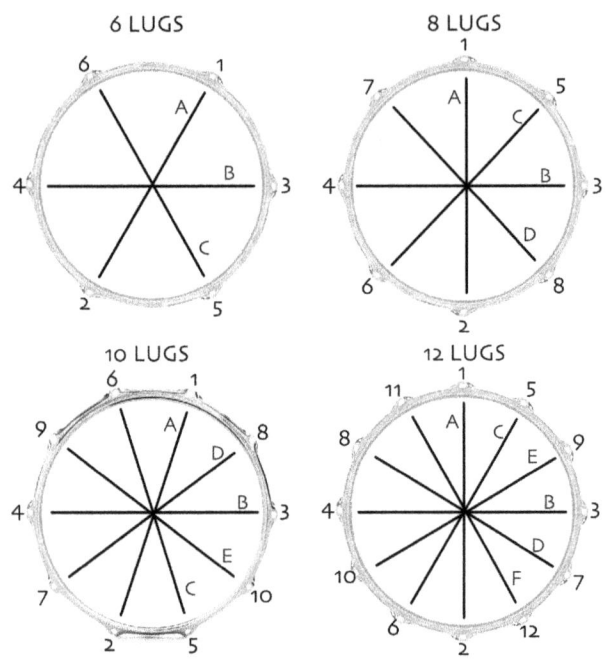

RULE #5 - Check how the drums sound in relation to each other, and adjust any pitches you want.

Toms should be noticeably different-sounding from each other, so it might be a good idea to start by tuning the lowest tom first (tune it to be fairly low-pitched) and move your way up in size from there.

RULE #6 - Bottom ('resonant') heads should generally be A LITTLE tighter than top ('batter') heads.

Resonant heads are thinner than batter heads, so they naturally tighten to a higher pitch. Plus this tuning relationship usually works well for making drums sound good.

ADDING MUFFLING TO YOUR DRUMS

One often-overlooked aspect of making drums sound good is controlling their sustain.

When drums have imperfect tuning and are allowed to ring free, they generally sound terrible, no matter how you play them. Even when well-tuned, sometimes drums just ring too long and/or excite the snare wires too much.

However, with a little muffling, the drums can sound great - you won't hear the imperfections in tuning as well, and the drums will sound more 'thumpy' and less resonant. For home practicing (and many styles of music), this tends to be ideal.

You can always experiment - but in case you want to use muffling, here are some guidelines.

TOMS AND SNARE

1) Add dampening to the outer edge of a drumhead. Moon-gels, Drumdots, and other similar products are great. You can also tape a patch of felt (or similar material) to the drumhead, which doesn't look as cool but also works. Back in the jazz era, drummers would often place their leather wallet on their snare (next to the hoop) at the beginning of a gig.

MOON-GEL PADS

2) For maximum thump, tune the drums to low pitches and add plenty of dampening material to the batter heads, such as 'o-rings' (flat rings of drumhead film).

BASS DRUM

1) Make sure you're using a decent quality bass drum head. Cheap bass drum heads sound a bit like hitting a metal baking sheet with a hammer. A good set of bass drum heads will transform your sound instantly and is a great investment.

2) Add a pillow or blanket (or similar) inside the drum, resting on the shell at the bottom so it touches both drumheads along their outer zones. (Try to avoid letting muffling touch the center area of a drumhead, generally).

3) Port holes in bass drum resonant heads are a good idea, especially for at-home practicing so you can adjust the muffling easily. They also help shorten the sustain of the drum by allowing air and sound to escape more rapidly.

BASS DRUM WITH PORT HOLE

GENERAL PRACTICE TIPS

PRACTICING IS IMPORTANT because your body has a **physical memory,** which is very different from (and learns a bit slower than) your cognitive memory. YOU MUST BE PATIENT while teaching yourself any physical pattern you want to play on the drums!

> "The more times in a row you do something the same way, the more your body can remember the action without your conscious mind."

Make sure to keep your 'PLAYING' and 'PRACTICING' separate, and spend time each week doing both. 'Playing' is good for having fun, but 'practicing' is what creates progress.

'**PLAYING**' is when you allow your drumming to be fun and expressive, maybe spontaneous and creative. It's when you are using drumming as a musical art form, or just simply enjoying doing stuff you already know how to do.

'**PRACTICING**' is when you repeat some unfamiliar action carefully, until it becomes easier and more familiar and you GAIN CONTROL. Also known as 'rehearsing'.

THE 'IDEAL PRACTICE METHOD'
for learning any pattern

1. Read and imagine the exercise.

Imagine what your body is about to do

2. Play one count at a time, slowly and in control - no mistakes!

At least four consecutive measures

3. Play / loop the exercise with correct timing / rhythm.

Keep tempo steady, and look away from the written music.

4. Explore various tempos.

Try playing faster than you think you can handle, you'll often be surprised!

5. Improve the pattern's quality and your physical actions to play it.

Listen to the exercise as you play it, and observe how it feels physically to play it.

HOW OFTEN TO PRACTICE?

CASUAL: 30 - 60 min per week

SERIOUS: 1-2 hours per week

PRO: 3+ hours per week

PART II: TRAINING

PLAY DRUMS NOW

THE ULTIMATE DRUMSET TRAINING PROGRAM

BASIC TECHNIQUE

GRIP / POSITIONING

CHECKPOINTS:

- Pinch 'fulcrum' of sticks (about 1/3 of the stick length from the bottom) between thumb and index finger. The back end of stick should extend beyond the side of your palm.

- Sit tall, look straight ahead
- Shoulders relaxed, deep breath
- Elbows close to sides, hanging down from your shoulders
- Wrists at least shoulder width apart, and 6-8" above playing surface (wrists should bend down slightly when sticks touch playing surface)

- Middle knuckles should ALWAYS stay lined up with your arms, for efficiency of the wrist joint.

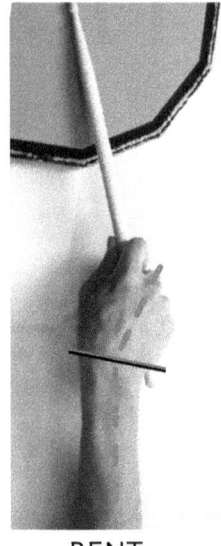 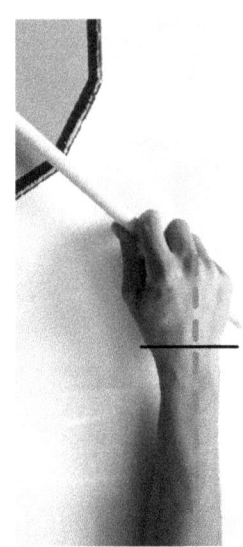

BENT   ALIGNED

- When you play, your body should stay in its position and just your wrists should bend like a flat hinge, to swing the sticks up or down.
- For positioning on your drumset, it's fine to use either your right or left hand for the hi-hat. There are pros and cons of both approaches, so try them both out and decide later.

LEFT ON HI-HAT   RIGHT ON HI-HAT

BASIC POSITIONING

- Sticks pointed together at about a 90° angle
- Palms down and pretty much flat (outside edge of hands can be angled downward a bit).

stick movement #1

THE REBOUND STROKE:

The REBOUND STROKE will help you to understand how the sticks behave naturally, so you can work WITH them (and let them do some of the work for you).

EX. #1 REBOUND STROKE INITIATION

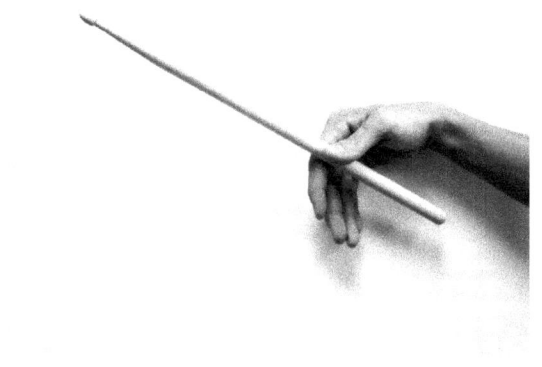

OPEN GRIP

GOAL: Increased awareness of natural rebound during all drumming.

SETTING: Practice pad, normal or heavy sticks, no metronome

TECHNIQUE: Open grip - simply hold the stick loosely at the fulcrum with thumb and forefinger, and keep the rest of your hand out of the way.

Start with both sticks at the top of the stroke (in the 'ceiling position').

<u>**ACTION #1:**</u> **For each stroke, swing the stick downward at the practice pad with a slight wrist movement,** and then KEEP YOUR WRIST STILL as the stick bounces off the practice pad.

Allow the stick to rebound, keeping your grip loose as you <u>let</u> the stick return to its original position. (This can be a bit tricky at first, don't give up!) Reset your positioning before the next stroke.

Repeat this stroke (with pauses in between) about 10-20 times in a row on each hand, until it is easy.

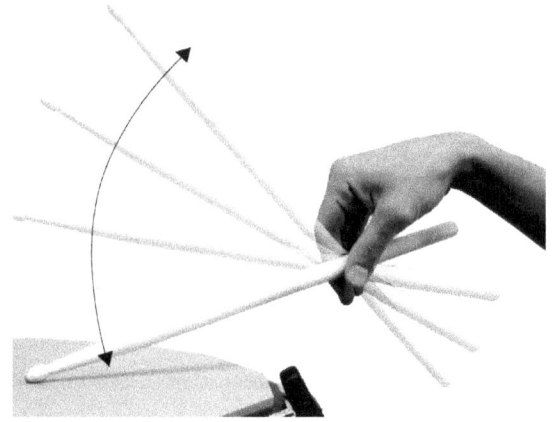

REBOUND STROKE

stick movement #2

THE FULL STROKE

The FULL STROKE is your primary drumming technique. It's the most efficient way to move your sticks around a drumset, and will provide you with plenty of control, speed, and power.

 EX. #2 FULL STROKE INITIATION

SETTING: Practice pad, normal or heavy sticks

TECHNIQUE: Closed grip, wrist control.

Set your 'ceiling position' to high volume for both sticks (approximately vertical).

ACTION #1: Practice 'full strokes' with each of the following patterns about 5-10 times in a row, maintaining perfect form until they are easy.

The movement should be a fast 'down-up' stroke, striking the pad and returning to the ceiling position immediately. There should be a moment when BOTH STICKS are motionless in the 'ceiling' position between every stroke. Make sure your grip stays closed.

    1. R,R,R,R   2. L,L,L,L   3. R,L,R,L

ACTION #2: 'tap' strokes - set your 'ceiling position' to low volume for both sticks (approximately 1" above the practice pad).

Repeat exercises 1-3 using the same 'down-up' technique as full strokes, but the 1" ceiling makes for more subtle movements - make sure to keep both sticks below 1" the whole time.

ACTION #3: Try the FULL STROKE movement on various parts of your drumset, one hand at a time, at various volumes. Keep your shoulders relaxed and elbows close to your sides. Do this exercise until both hands are familiar with the various positions around your kit.

- **TIP #1:** Your GOAL here is for the 'full stroke' to be your DEFAULT MOVEMENT, your natural tendency during all drumming.

- **TIP #2:** Make each movement as short as possible. If you blink during one of these full strokes, you shouldn't see evidence that any movement happened!

Start at 'ceiling position' | Quick DOWN-STROKE | Immediate UP-STROKE

  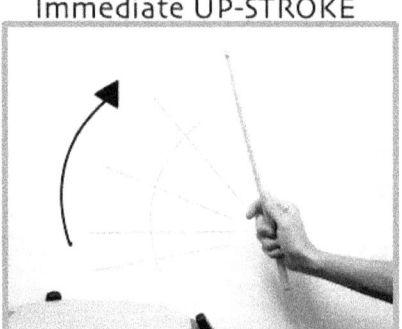

return to ceiling position

stick movement #3

ALTERNATING STROKES

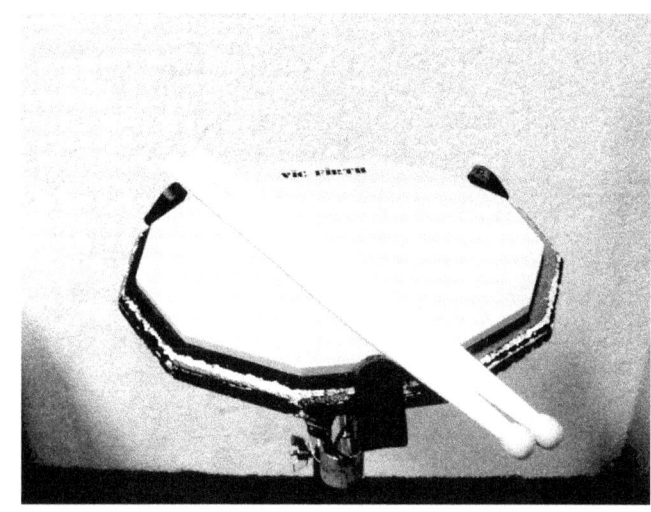

'**Alternating strokes**' (R,L,R,L,R...etc.) is BY FAR the most common action in drumming. You will want to achieve perfection and speed with this style, for each of the strokes you've just learned.

 EX. #3 ALTERNATING STROKES
INITIATION

SETTING: Practice pad, normal or heavy sticks

TECHNIQUE: Closed grip, wrist control.

REMEMBER TO STAY RELAXED! THIS HELPS YOUR SKILLS IMPROVE QUICKLY.

ACTION #1: Using full strokes, play continuously alternating R,L,R,L,R... etc, starting at a slow speed, for about 1-2 minutes.

- Keep good positioning
- Maintain equal volume between your hands
- Experiment with various speeds and volume levels

ACTION #2: 'ALTERNATING RUNS' (shown at right) >>
Play short bursts of alternating notes, <u>pausing after each burst</u> to make sure your sticks are both motionless in the 'ceiling' position.

ALTERNATING 'RUNS'

1
```
  1 2 3
||: ♩ ♩ ♩ 𝄽 𝄽 𝄽 :||
   R L R
   L R L
```

2
```
  1 2 3 4 5
||: ♩ ♩ ♩ ♩ ♩ 𝄽 𝄽 𝄽 :||
   R L R L R
   L R L R L
```

3
```
  1 2 3 4 5 6 7
||: ♩ ♩ ♩ ♩ ♩ ♩ ♩ 𝄽 :||
   R L R L R L R
   L R L R L R L
```

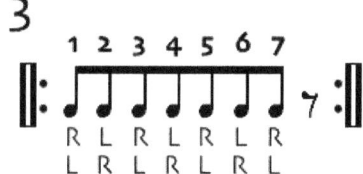

4
```
  1 2 3 4 5 6 7 8 9
||: ♩ ♩ ♩ ♩ ♩ ♩ ♩ ♩ ♩ 𝄽 :||
   R L R L R L R L R
   L R L R L R L R L
```

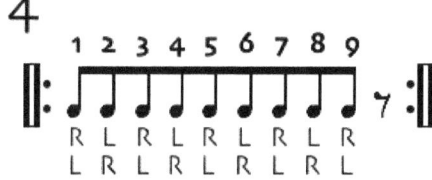

pedal movement #1:

THE 'RESTING FOOT' STROKE

EX. #4 RESTING FOOT STROKE INITIATION

The **RESTING FOOT STROKE** is a guaranteed way to achieve full control of your bass drum pedal. Essentially, you execute a backswing right BEFORE each stroke, and then pause the beater close to the head.

In between notes played on the bass drum, you allow your foot's weight to rest completely on the pedal board.

This stroke is the only good choice for your technique during your development of skills on the drums, and is efficient enough to be used as **your primary technique** for the rest of your drumming life.

This technique is necessary, because the spring on a bass drum pedal is the only source of power for the backswing, so you need to keep it stretched so you can use it at any time.

SETTING: Drumset, foot on bass drum pedal, no metronome

TECHNIQUE: Entire foot stays in contact with pedal board during movements. (This is important during early training to develop ankle control, but other techniques can be used later.)

START with your foot resting on the pedal board, so the beater is 1" or so off the head.

ACTION #1: Execute a backswing and strike, as one quick movement. Let the beater bounce off the head, but then immediately steady its movement about 1" away from the drumhead and allow your foot to rest again.

- Try to create maximum backswing with this technique. You should feel a 'whiplash' effect on the bass drum beater, when executing this technique properly.

ACTION #2: Play these patterns (below), making sure to return to 'resting position' at the end of each group of notes (play each group quickly so the beater stays in motion during the group). Take as much time as you need between groups, to use proper form.

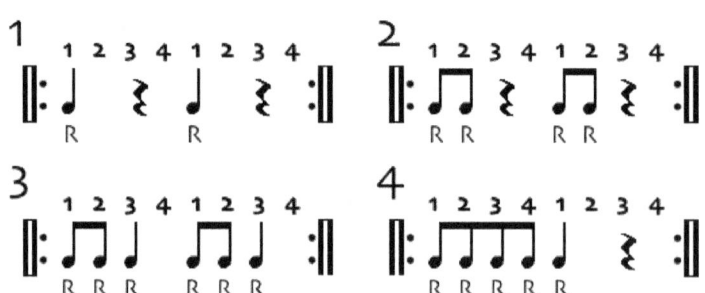

24

pedal movement #2:

THE HI-HAT CHICK

EX. #5 HI-HAT CHICK INITIATION

The **'HI-HAT CHICK'** is the main control method for the hi-hat pedal. Essentially, you keep the pedal pressed all the way down at the end of each stroke, and wait until just before the next stroke to lift it, so the movements are sharp.

Eventually, this technique will be the foundation for techniques like the hi-hat 'bark' and 'splash'.

SETTING: Drumset, hi-hats set to about 1" apart resting distance, foot on hi-hat pedal, no metronome

TECHNIQUE: Entire foot stays in contact with pedal board during movements.

<u>**ACTION #1**</u>: **Press your foot on the pedal** to keep the hi-hat cymbals closed tightly. This is your hi-hat foot's default position.

<u>**ACTION #2**</u>: **Lift and close the top cymbal as one quick movement,** to create a 'chick' sound, leaving the cymbals closed at the end.

(TIP: don't let the top cymbal come all the way up or the hardware will make a noise when it hits the top of its range.)

<u>**ACTION #3**</u>: **Play these patterns below,** making sure every note has a nice sharp 'chick' sound (go slowly):

INTRO TO DRUM RUDIMENTS

INSTRUCTIONS: PRE-RUDIMENT SKILLS

(exercises on next page)

'Drum rudiments' (see https://en.wikipedia.org/wiki/Drum_rudiment) are a collection of 40 short drumming phrases, that are grouped in four families of 'skill':

1- rolls   2- paradiddles   3- flams   4- drags

These four techniques create special sounds and textures on drums (or any percussion), that you can use to decorate your playing.

These 'rudimental' skills originated as a way to make one drum sound more interesting, which was especially useful when a drummer would be traveling on foot and carrying a drum by a strap over their shoulder, for example when accompanying a military.

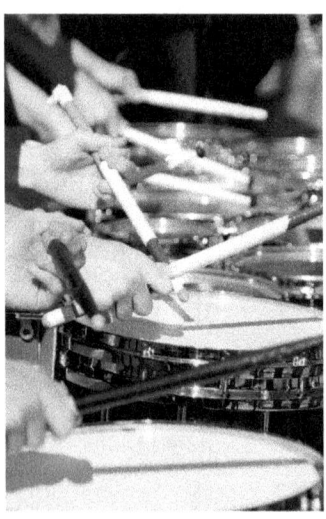

Examples of this style of drumming are easy to find in snare solos and any music played by modern drumlines… but the rudiments are also widely used by **skilled drumset players** (and many other types of drummers around the world).

Drum rudiments have often been treated as the foundation of drumming skill, and teachers often include them as one of the first steps in training. They are sometimes difficult to master but give you a wealth of expressivity on the drumset!

 **ROUND 1) During the linear sticking patterns,** try to let your stick bounce twice on each double 'R' or 'L'. In other words, your wrist should make one movement down, wait for the stick to bounce twice, then return to its original height. (tip: hold the stick loosely, as shown in the instructions for the **'rebound stroke'.**

Use **full strokes** for all other notes.

 **ROUND 2) During the layered sticking patterns,** use full strokes for all notes. Notes marked with 'T' should be played at the same moment so they sound like one note. This will build your coordination skills for playing two rhythms at once on a drumset, which is helpful during complex grooves and fills.

These patterns will also prepare you for learning the **'flam rudiments'.** (A 'flam' is a regular note played by one hand, with a quieter note played by the opposite hand slightly earlier but almost at the same time.)

FLAMS

L R   R L

R = right hand
L = left hand
T = together
    (both hands)

PRE-RUDIMENT SKILLS

LINEAR STICKING PATTERNS

1 Double stroke / drag (R)*

R R L _ R R L _

2 Double stroke / drag (L)*

L L R _ L L R _

3 Double stroke roll

R R L L R R L L

4 Paradiddle

R L R R L R L L

LAYERED STICKING PATTERNS

5

T R T R

6

T L T L

7 Flam tap*

T R T L T R T L

8

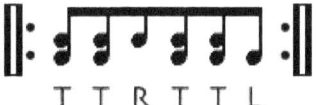

T T R T T L

9 Swiss army triplet (R)*

T R L T R L

10 Swiss army triplet (L)*

T L R T L R

*NOTE: Most of these are not accurate notation of specific rudiments, but they will help you practice skills that allow you to learn the rudiments more easily.

RHYTHMS AND READING

TYPICAL DRUMSET NOTATION

If you're looking at any sheet music, method books, transcriptions found on the internet or in publications etc, THIS is what you'll likely encounter:

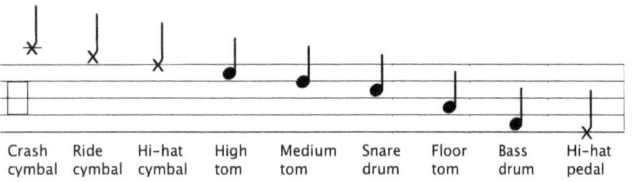

This notation works, and is very common so you should learn to read this style. However, the Play Drums Now material uses a slightly different legend that makes drumming music clearer to read.

The main difference is that the tom note-heads are clear and therefore easy to tell apart from the snare notes, and they are lower in the staff rather than separated above and below the snare row.

(Normally, clear noteheads are reserved for 'half-notes' and 'whole notes', but since drumset music usually has no need for those sizes, it's not a problem to change the meaning of that notehead within this training program.)

READING DRUM NOTATION IN THE 'PLAY DRUMS NOW' BOOKS

All **PRACTICE PAD EXERCISES** in the Play Drums Now training materials use this key:

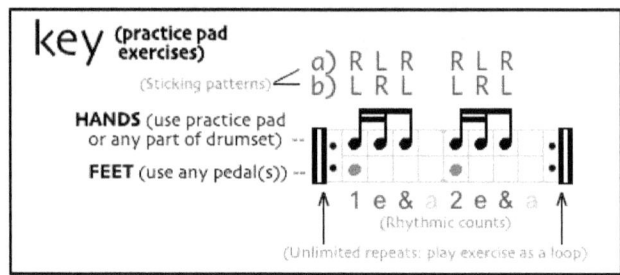

All **DRUMSET EXERCISES** use this key:

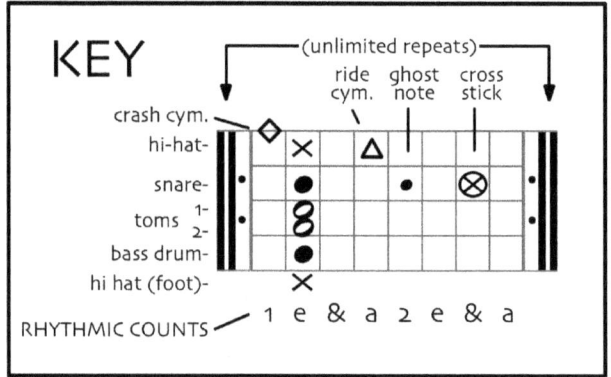

THE GRID / STAFF

This is used to make it easy to see the spacing of the rhythms in music.

UNLIMITED REPEATS

The 'repeat bars' at the beginning and end of most patterns in this book are meant to be 'unlimited', so you repeat/loop the pattern as many times as you want without stopping. (Usually repeat signs mean 'play the section twice, then continue on'.)

NOTES AND RESTS - THE 'ALPHABET' OF RHYTHM NOTATION

Think of notes and rests like bricks of different lengths, that get packed next to each other in a measure to make rhythm. They are measured as fractions of a 'whole note' - like parts of an inch on a ruler.

'Triplet' notes are 3 evenly spaced notes/rests in the area that only 2 would normally fit. These are designated by a '3' displayed over the notes/rests. It's also possible to create 'quintuplets', 'sextuplets', and other '-tuplets' by adding other numbers over a group of notes.

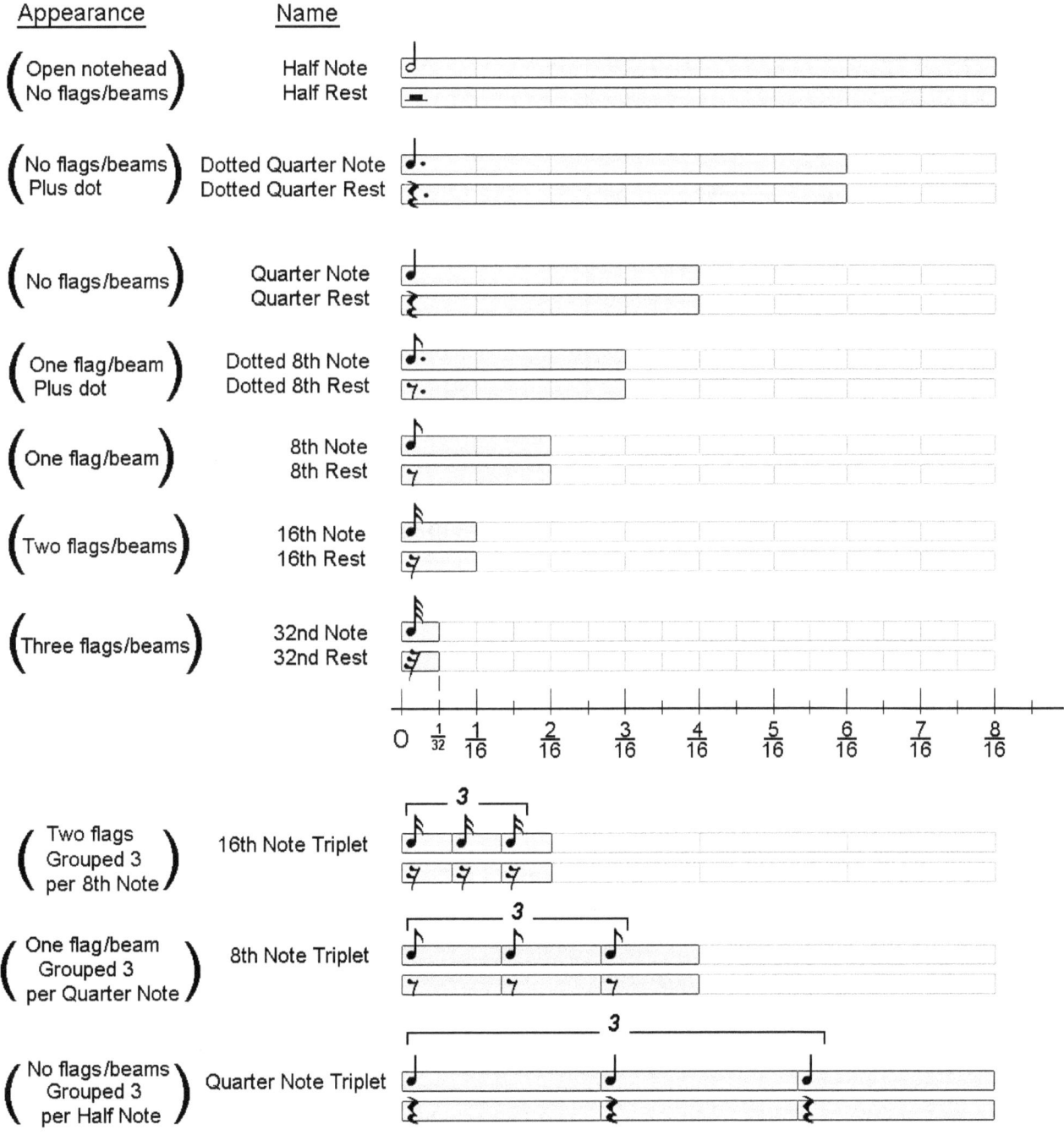

*Whole notes are not shown because (a) the scale of this image would be greatly compressed and (b) drummers rarely see whole notes in their music.

HOW NOTES + RESTS MAKE RHYTHMS

The note and rest 'bricks' (previous page) can be packed next to each other in any combinations within a measure, <u>to create a rhythm out of the notes</u>.

Written notes are usually connected in groups to make reading easier.

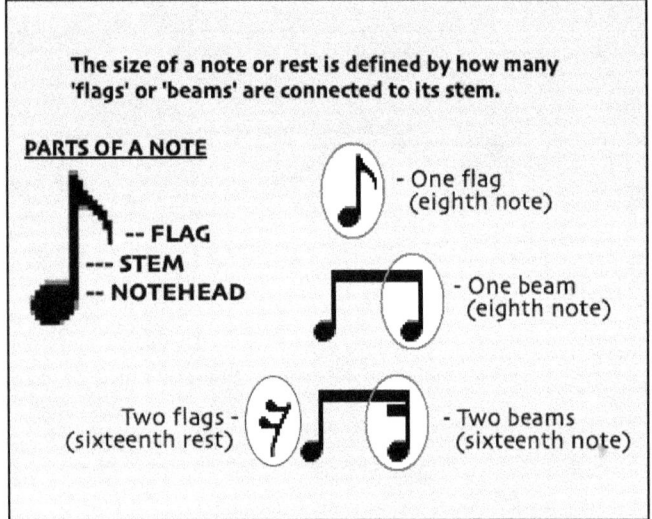

Just Hit The Beginning Of The Note

Drummers have a special relationship with rhythms: we usually can't control how long our notes last, while almost all other instruments can.

So when playing written music, we just strike the drum / cymbal / etc. at the beginning of each note and wait until the next one, no matter how long the actual note is - whether it's an 8th note or a 16th note, it's still just one impact.

Most other instruments have to make sure to control the length of their sound according to the note size.

PLAYING RHYTHMS IN THIS BOOK

For the exercises in this book, you won't REALLY need to know how to read music yet - just

1) count the squares in the grid evenly, and

2) play on any counts that have a note in that box. For example, this rhythm will sound like a 'door knock' rhythm when played correctly:

O		O	O	O		O	
1	2	3	4	5	6	7	8

MORE INFO ON READING

This information is just a brief intro to notation.

More in-depth reading instructions can be found in book 2 of the LEVEL 2 training series: **'Play Drums Now 2.2: Rhythms and Timing'.**

For now, we'll just start with some practice on a few basic 8th note rhythms and 16th note rhythms.

INSTRUCTIONS:
BASIC RHYTHMS

(exercises on next page)

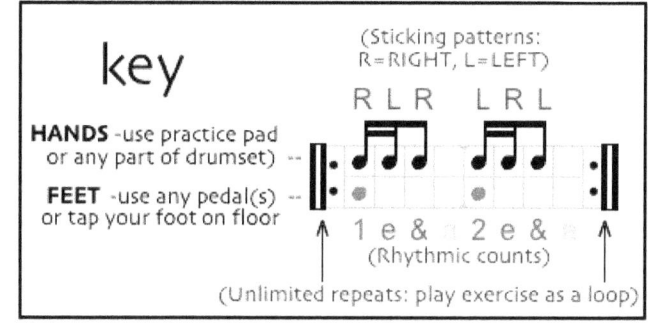

 **ROUND 1: Slowly speak the rhythmic counts from left to right** while playing the notes in the rhythm on the appropriate counts. Use alternating sticking (R,L,R,L or L,R,L,R etc.)

Play / loop each rhythm at a constant speed, at least 4 times in a row without stopping. (Make sure not to leave any extra space between the last count of one measure and the first count of the next.)

If / when you can hear and remember the sound of the rhythm while playing it, you can try looking away from the music and playing by ear, rather than counting.

Explore various speeds and volume levels to see what each rhythm sounds like in different conditions.

ROUND 2: Add the 'pulse note' with one of your feet. Play these rhythms according to the instructions above, while also playing the grey 'pulse note' with either your RF or LF.

Even if you can only play the pulse note with some of these rhythms, that's still awesome - it will help build your coordination and timing skills!

PLAY DRUMS NOW
THE ULTIMATE DRUMSET TRAINING PROGRAM

8TH NOTE RHYTHMS

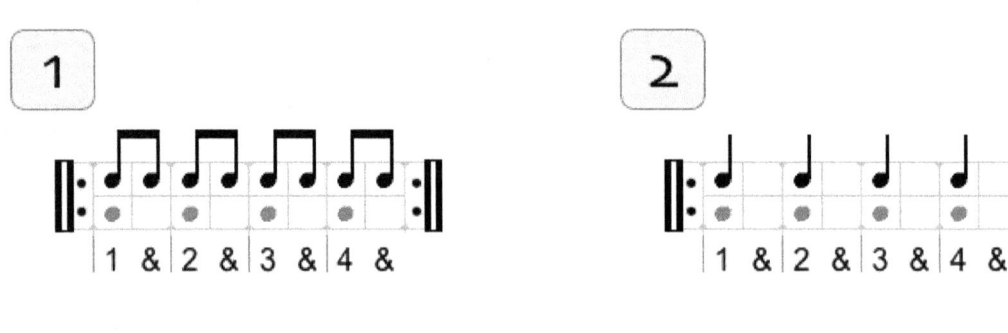

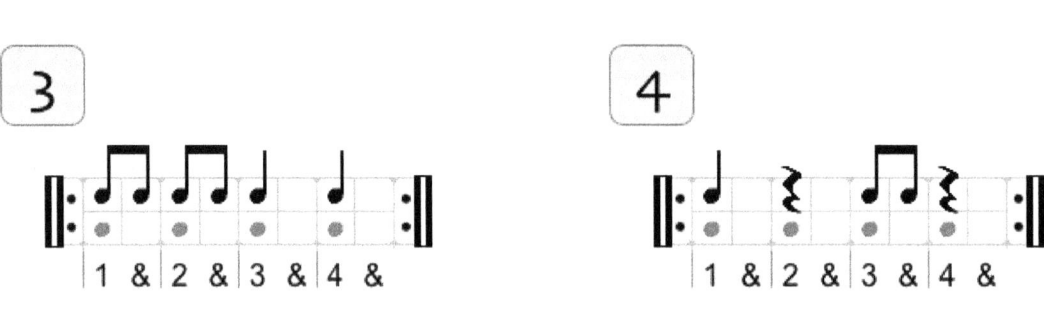

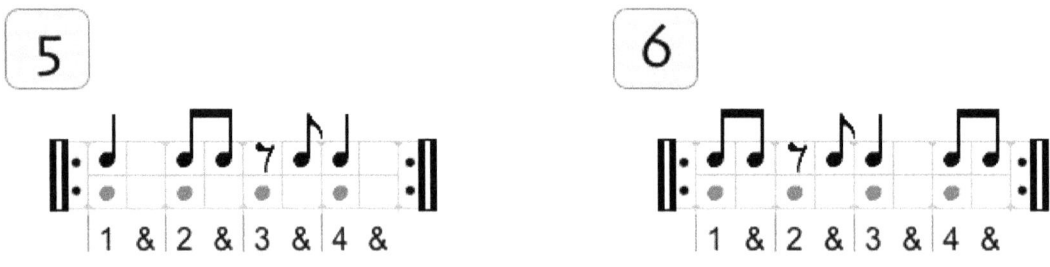

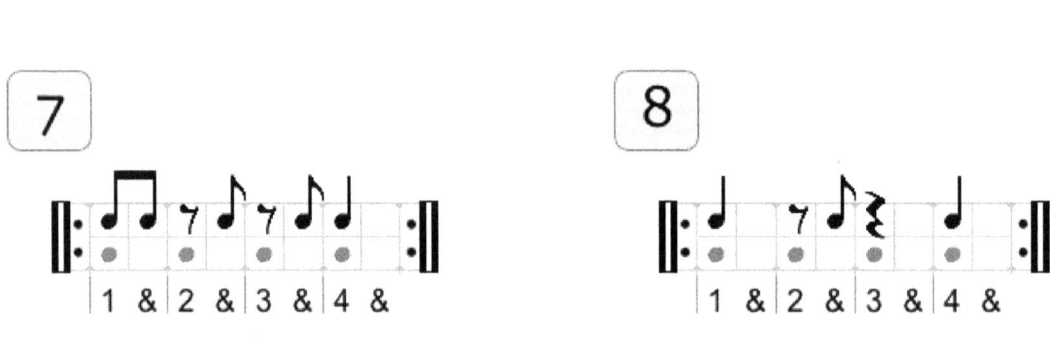

16TH NOTE RHYTHMS

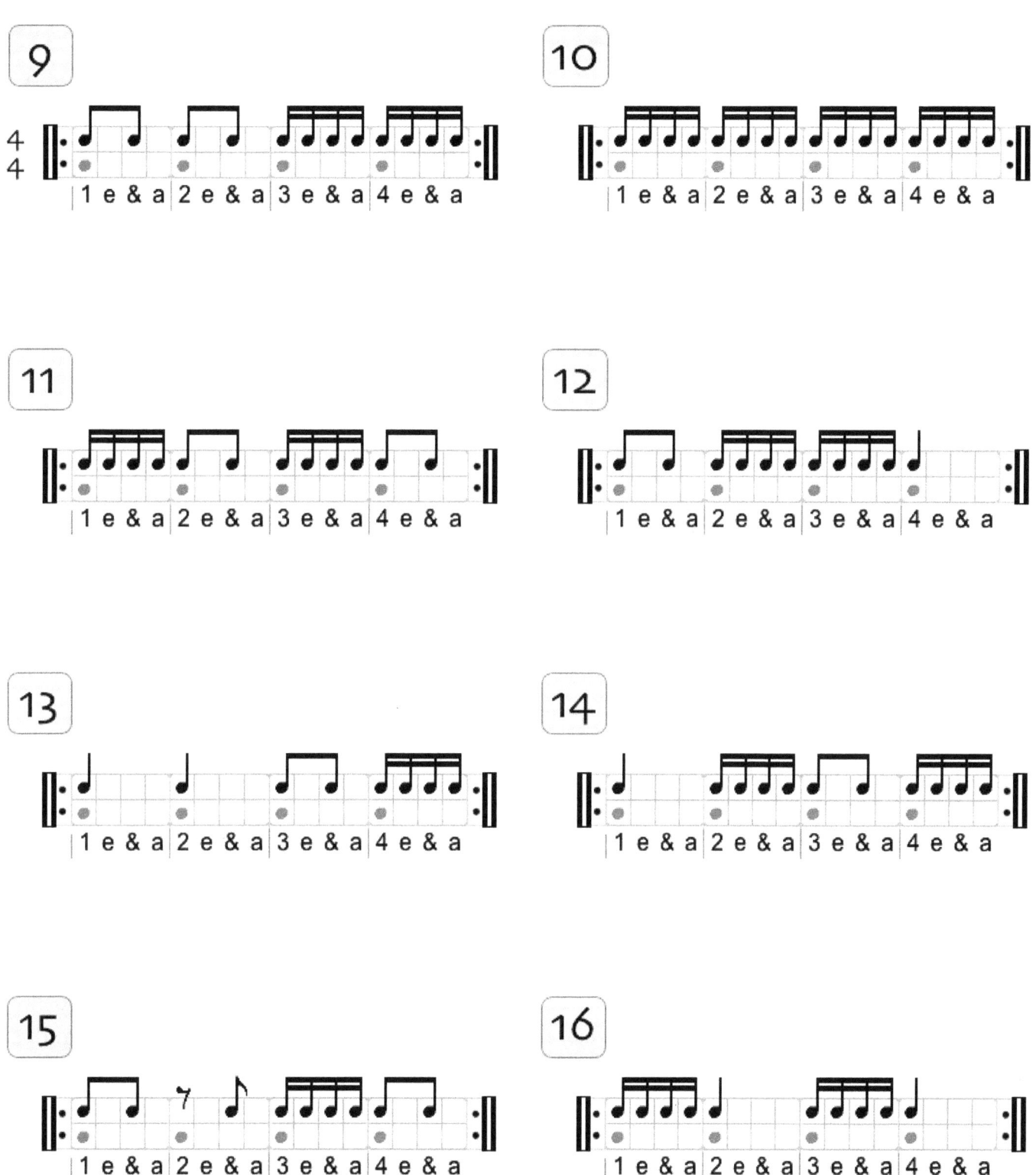

GROOVE BASICS

GROOVES ARE THE MAIN ACTION USED IN DRUMMING, so they might be the most important part of your vocabulary as a drummer.

Be really careful when you're learning any groove, to make sure you're playing it right. Go slowly enough that you don't make ANY mistakes! Repeated enough times accurately, your body will absorb the sequence of movements, and it'll start feeling easy. THEN you you will be able to speed it up.

HOW TO LEARN GROOVES REALLY FAST = DON'T MAKE ANY MISTAKES!

The only reason mistakes happen is impatience or lack of focus, neither of which is a good enough excuse to frustrate yourself when learning a groove.

RIGHT OR LEFT ON HI-HAT?

LH on hi-hat   RH on hi-hat

You can play the hi-hat with either hand and still end up as a great drummer. There are advantages and disadvantages to both approaches, so you may want to try each of them and decide later.

One main consideration is that no matter how you play grooves on the hi-hats, you'll want to be comfortable **playing the ride with your right hand.** This is because the ride cymbal is usually positioned on the right side of the drumsets you'll encounter when playing at schools, venues, etc. It's not always convenient to rearrange those drumsets to get the ride on your left, so you'll probably want to adapt to the usual territory.

Many drummers play the hi-hat with their right hand mainly so they don't have to switch hands when switching cymbals. Others (including me and many of my students) don't mind learning to play both ways, because playing the hi-hat left-handed is a much less hindering position to be in.

You can always change your mind, so feel free to experiment with the options first!

DRUMSET TARGETS

HOW TO HIT A DRUM OR CYMBAL:

"...like you mean it."

GENERALLY, you want your sticks to bounce quickly off surfaces upon impact, so you don't mute their sound. Keep your grip relaxed during impact, and/or lift the stick right after the moment the impact.

Following through or using too much force can damage or break your equipment!

DRUM SOUND-ZONES

Each drum can produce several sounds, depending on where / how you strike it:

- center sound
- outer-drumhead sound (overtone)
- rim-click
- cross-stick
- rimshot
- stick shot
- mute stroke
    ...and more.

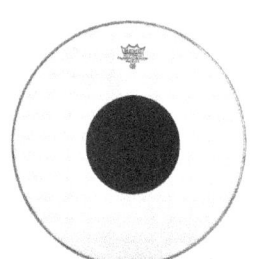

Don't worry about all those yet - for now, just focus on the **center sound** and aim for a 3"-4" circle-shaped target in the middle of each drum.

CYMBAL SOUND-ZONES

Each cymbal has 3 main targets to aim for: the 'ride' sound, the 'bell' sound, and the 'crash' sound.

'Ride' sound: tip of stick strikes anywhere on wide area ('bow') of cymbal.

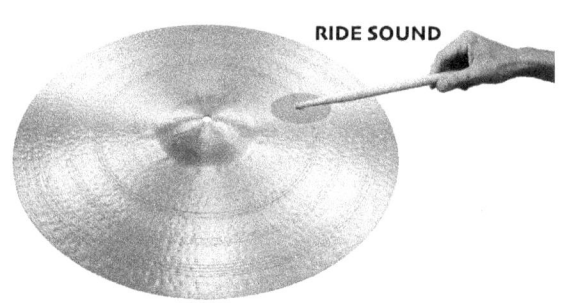

'Bell' sound: shoulder of stick strikes on center bell of cymbal (explore placement to find best sound).

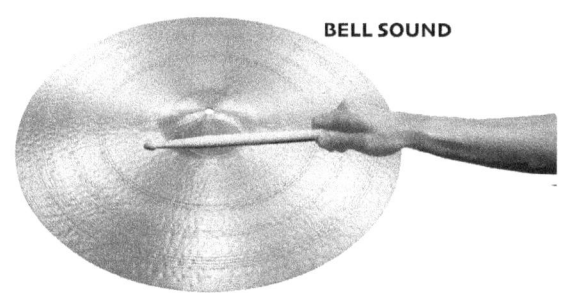

'Crash' sound: shoulder of stick strikes edge of cymbal, ideally slightly off-center from the point on the cymbal closest to you, or in a glancing motion.

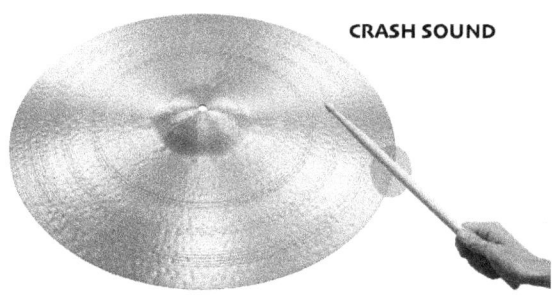

INSTRUCTIONS: DRUMSET GROOVES

(exercises on next page)

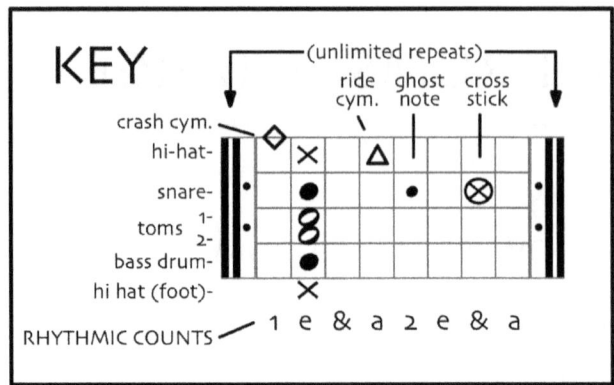

 **ROUND 1: Play through the groove carefully,** reading from left to right. Hit any notes together that are stacked above each other.

At first, you don't have to play the groove at a steady rate - just make sure you play every part of the sequence correctly, at least a few times in a row, until it feels manageable to play.

Then, maintain a constant speed, and play / loop the groove **at least 4 times in a row** without stopping. (If that is challenging, go much slower - it should be easy, so pick a speed that seems 'too easy' at first. Make sure you can play 4 consecutive measures accurately (no mistakes) before trying faster speeds.

Then, keep looping the groove and explore some different tempos!

 **ROUND 3: Substitute a crash cymbal for the first hi-hat note,** (A) every measure, (B) every 2 measures, (C) every 4 measures.

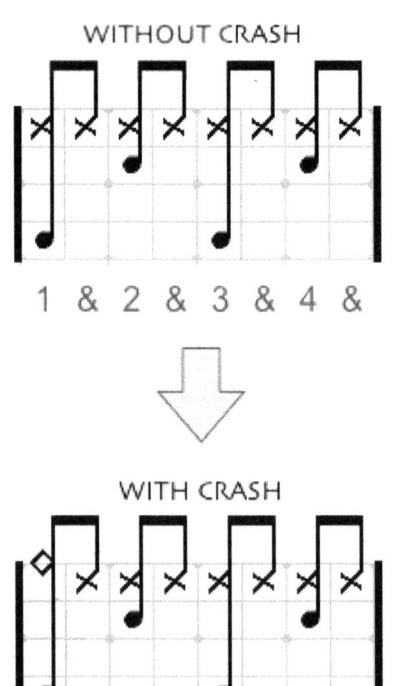

 **ROUND 2: Play the grooves' hi-hat rhythm on different surfaces,** like your ride cymbal, lowest tom, etc.

Explore various speeds and volume levels to make the grooves sound the best.

8TH NOTE GROOVES

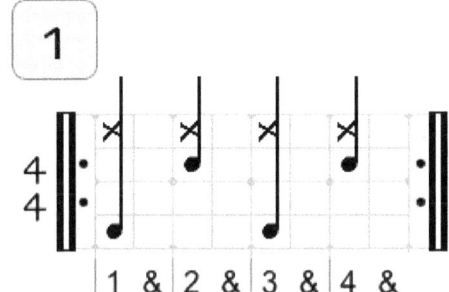

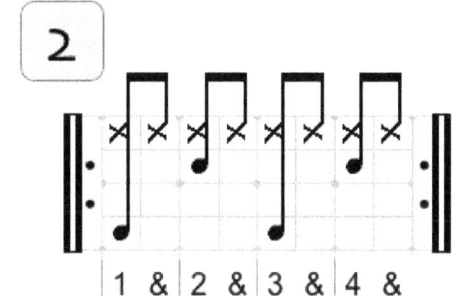

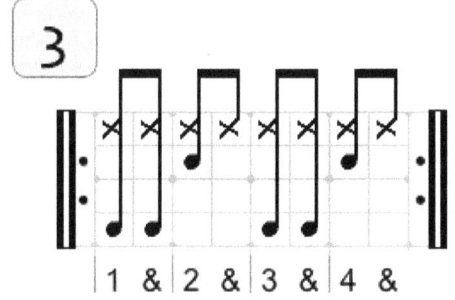

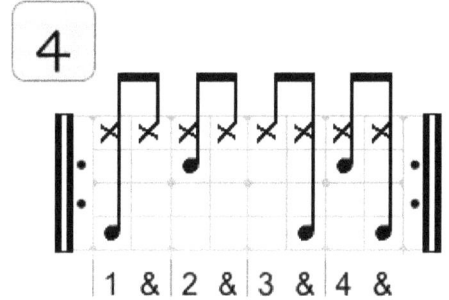

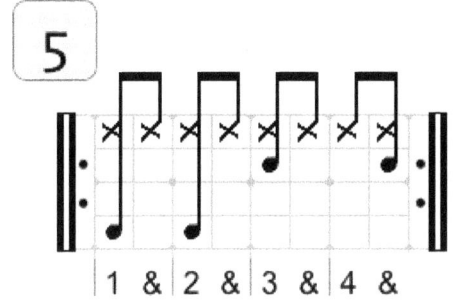

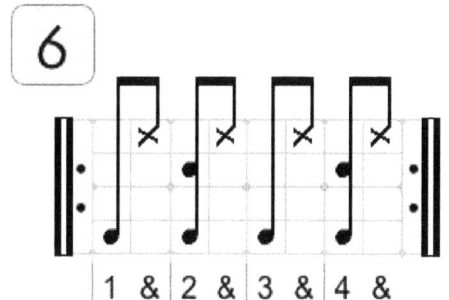

FILLS AND DRUM LOOPS

TIP:

Most of these fills are designed to work well when played with alternating strokes, leading with your RH. (i.e. R,L,R,L...) This will also make it easy to hit the crash with your right hand.

WHAT ARE FILLS?

Fills are essentially decorations, usually added to grooves in significant moments of the music. Often fills happen right before a song changes between any two sections of its structure, such as from a verse to a chorus.

A drummer's job is to have plenty of these fills in their vocabulary, so that when there's a moment in music that needs a fill, the drummer can choose one (or invent one) that sounds good and play it easily.

This section of training starts with several fills for you to learn, and then shows you how to combine them with a groove!

INSTRUCTIONS:
FILLS AND DRUM LOOPS

(exercises on next page)

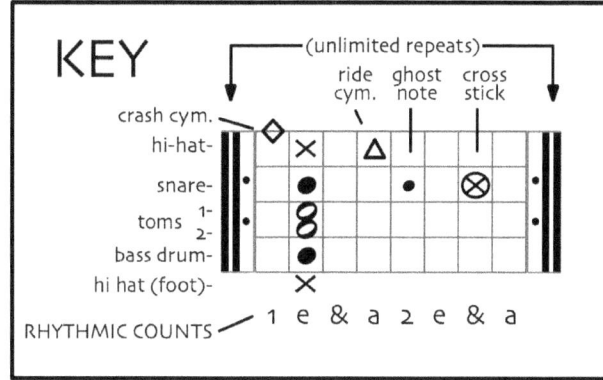

 **ROUND 1: Play through the '8th and 16th note fills' carefully,** with alternating R,L,R,L strokes, and hit the crash at the end with your right hand.

Practice each fill until you are comfortable with the flow of movement around the drums - try to be as relaxed as possible every time you play it, so the movements become more efficient. This will allow you to speed up.

Repeat each fill many times, to gain speed as well as to memorize these fills to some degree, for the next step.

ROUND 3: Play each combination of groove and fill consecutively, with no breaks in between. You can go in any order that you wish, and it's good to change up the order and repeat this exercise a few times.

It may be helpful at first to do this exercise with twice or more on each fill, before going to the next.

ROUND 2: Practice the 'Groove / Fill Loops' one at a time, to make sure each combination of the groove and fill works well and sounds right. Repeat enough times to be comfortable with each combination.

PLAY DRUMS NOW
THE ULTIMATE DRUMSET TRAINING PROGRAM

8TH + 16TH NOTE FILLS

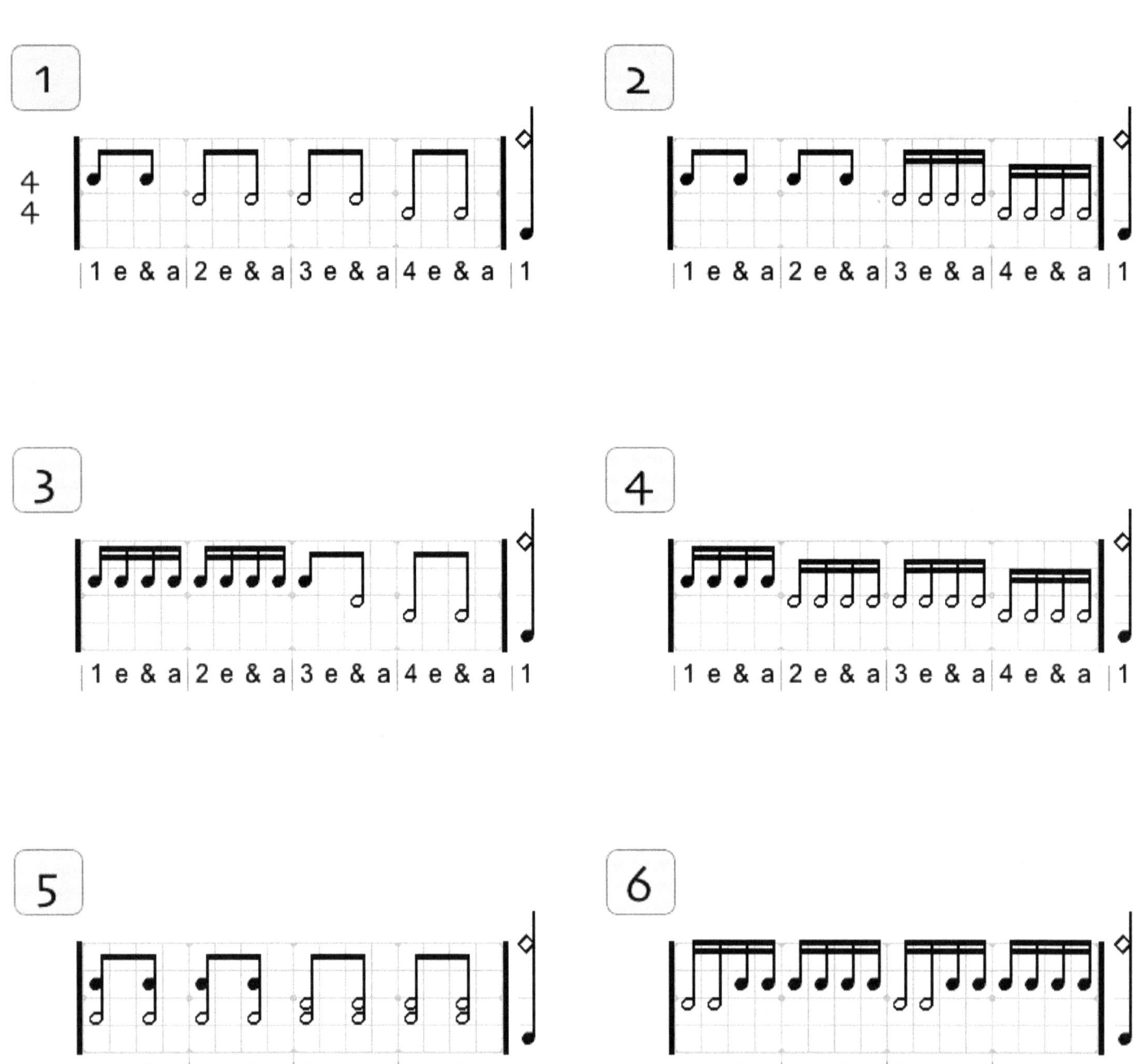

GROOVE / FILL LOOPS

Did you complete this book?

CONGRATS!!!

NICE WORK.

SKILLS ASSESSMENT:

Check these criteria to see if you're ready to move on from this book!

- You understand the knowledge and wisdom in the written sections of this book

- You have experienced an increase in skill from training with this material

- You can play any of the exercises in this book at a comfortable tempo

- You feel confident in your ability to learn and play new similar material

- You are motivated to learn more and become a better drummer

NEXT STEPS:

- **Continue on to the LEVEL 2 MATERIALS!!** You are now at an INTERMEDIATE status of training.

- Go to www.PlayDrumsNow.com for more resources.

ABOUT THE AUTHOR:

Adam Randall - Drummer, educator, and author. Adam has performed and recorded drums professionally with bands across various styles. His career in drum instruction started with ten years at the Colorado Music Institute, and he has since been teaching at Klash Drums in MN. He published his first books on drum instruction in 2010, and he continues to create new materials as part of his mission to make it easier for people to become great drummers.

Follow @playdrumsnow on Instagram, facebook, twitter, youtube etc. for more!

www.ingramcontent.com/pod-product-compliance
Lightning Source LLC
Chambersburg PA
CBHW050456110426
42743CB00017B/3392